A Doorkeeper
in the House

A Doorkeeper in the House

Victor Depta

Ion Books
P.O. Box 111327
Memphis, TN 38111-1327

Ion Books
P.O. Box 111327
Memphis, Tennessee 38111-1327

Library of Congress Cataloging-in-Publication Data

Depta, Victor.
    A doorkeeper in the house / Victor Depta.
      p. cm.
    ISBN 0-938507-21-4 : $10.95
    1. Family--Southern States--Poetry.   I. Title.
    PS3554.E64D65   1993
    811' .54--dc20   93-3560
                                                    CIP

Acknowledgements

Grateful acknowledgement is made to the editors of the following publications in which these poems have appeared:

Appalachian Journal: "Cousin Michael's Trip, Section 22" (printed as "The Glittering")
The Beloit Poetry Journal: "The Foyer"
The Black Cat: "Juke Boxes"
The Cape Rock: "The Antiquity of the Muse" ("Saraghina") and "When Possibility Is a
    Gesture" ("Old Crow")
The Centennial Review: "Cousin Michael and the Hognose Snake" and "Strange Hope"
The Georgia Review: "The Embroidery Sampler" ("The Embroidery")
Graham House Review: "Sacrifice the Moon" ("Colleen")
Kentucky Poetry Review: "It Didn't Come from Hallmark"
Louisville Review: "The Mad Whore of Peach Tree" ("The Bean Sprouts")
Memphis State Review: "The Confusions of Eros" ("The Basketball Coach") and
    "The Sanctified Lizard" ("Bible Class")
The Miscellany: A Davidson Review: "Cousin Michael's Trip, Sections 7 and 14" ("The
    Field, 6-7-9")
Mississippi Valley Review: "Cousin Michael's Trip, Section 30" ("Limited War")
The Ohio Review: "Like One Indentured" ("Peach Galls")
Oyez Review: "Hypocrites of Redemption"
Poem: "Where the Pines Groom Heaven," "The Fever of Every House" and
    "The Club and the Harley"
Shenandoah: "Selene's Tea" ("Selene")
Studia Mystica: "Uncle Walter Chatting with Wilde" ("Holding Court")
Webster Review: "The Winged Mule" ("The Four Mice")
West Branch: "The Sympathetic Rib" ("Adam and Eve")

"The Egotism of Death" first appeared in *The Chariton Review* (Spring 1985).
"Entering the Priesthood" first appeared in *The California Quarterly,*
    Copyright 1987 by The Regents of the University of California.

Cover illustration by Nancy Clift Spicer
Book design by David Spicer and Nancy Clift Spicer

CONTENTS

Cousin Michael

Grandfather

Aunt Thelma

The Foyer

I think people have glue on them, or explode. They put on
      clothes and hair and eyes like wearing furniture, and
      I've got a trigger on my face. I worry about people seeing
      my left cheek rise and fall back like it was shooting at
      them.

What a messy foyer with aunt Thelma and my sister Charlene,
      uncle Walter and Grandfather, along with fourteen
      cousins and some other poor relations except
      my mother–she never comes to visit–illiterates my
      Grandfather says about people like her, trash the soul
      struggles out of a ditch from like honeysuckle.

I don't like that. He doesn't understand what makes her and
      the relatives on her side dull-shiny and smooth like
      an old quarter, and makes them know a vending machine
      for sure when they see one coming.

Anyway, I know I'm a ghost in the foyer, one of those kind with
      a floating tongue and shocked chainless. I know where
      everybody is and drift to the door for Grandfather when
      the doorbell rings.

I boo greetings and see that look in their eyes saying *so this
      is how he turned out, the dope head. I figured this
      would happen. I wonder if he's got herpes yet, the
      drunk.* And I hug my relations and kiss them on the
      cheek.

The Mad Whore of Peach Tree

So you're here to visit your aunt Thelma. Who amongst
them told you I was mad, or did you simply think of me,
    and come?
Ah, little nephew, the years stagger by so fast.
You were the sweetest, handsomest; but you hunkered past
us like a stray dog with a puzzled look, and so obedient!
I sighed, more than once, at the way you were shunted
off and made to sleep like a boarder among your cousins.

I'm not crazy, now, but boringly sane as the new hens
in the gravel. Did you notice them? I had to pen
the cat up for a month. How could she get it in her head
that they weren't yellow mice? So not a one is dead.
You should see them fly–like chickadees with the dropsy–
to the chestnut trees and cluck like feathery hulls
when the pups quarrel. More coffee, child? What a dull
subject, for you, to have come this far to bear with.

Enough of chickens. I was all spring the mad whore
of Peach Tree. God exposed himself everywhere.
He talked from the twigs of trees with his green mouth
and uncovered his sex the first time to me in the bean sprouts.
He was showing off the tip of his first leaves
like an adolescent boy, how innocent! who unsheathes
it on his stem with unbearable tenderness.

Have they told you, yet, how I ran about the hills
like a crazy ballad? Moss or a mushroom sent me reeling
from ridge to ridge; and let me tell you, more than a few
of the ladies at our church would bless me had I fallen at a pew,
rigid and dumb as a board, and not in a stinking ditch.
But God didn't call me to church. I guess I was the witch
with a rake and hoe. I certainly made beans grow.

But I learned this, child, about God:
my heart so pumps with need, that if I throbbed
with Him, we'd hurl, one being, groom and bride,
like stones, and crash amid the stirring of birds,
to join the colloquy of sunrise astir with wings.
We'd cause a flap of havoc; dawn would fling
itself into the air and reel in panic at so much joy.

Where in that happy chaos would be the soul,
and the body with its meat and bones, cupped as a watery bowl
around its being? Would I, a black snake, gulp down
the fledglings on the hill–leaf, branch and tree–devour
the sky, also, and then engorge, like that old ring of fire, the sun,
love's serpent mouth and tail, while mockingbird and thrush
cry in the wilderness without their broods?

I'm quite sane, now, and I've visited your grandmother's grave.
The irises you planted–I know you planted them, so save
yourself a protest–have done very well, both the violet
and the yellow ones with the brown speckles near the lip.
I'm keeping after Marvin. I have to pay the little brute
to mow the grass up there, and take the scythe to the brush.

And now the leaves, little nephew, humped on their points,
skitter in the road before me like grotesque crabs.
They scurry, in the chill wind, to the weeds and underbrush,
and hiss like embittered serpents to the waning sun
that paradise is finally, now, undone.

The Embroidery Sampler

Aunt Thelma said: these are from my sampler.
You see, in this embroidery, how the stem
arcs up from its leafy tangle and then leans–
the blossom is quite a show, don't you think
blent as it is with the next stem–and so on
as they caper in a lively run continually
though you can't tell from the sample.

I'd like to put them in a book, the way you do your poems
or like old printers did the initial letter
to show that I, an ancient widow fretting with her threads
can stitch a gloss on any text of God's, now that I see
my loss was greater while my husband lived
than is this fetter of loneliness.

I could sit back, I suppose, and grieve about the dead
who come and go, whispering all sorts of nonsense.
I've stitched on linen all the fine sentiments:
wet-eyed aphorisms for my brothers' wives,
cornucopias, circles of rosemary, dill and thyme
but lately, I have original designs

as you can see from the coverlets and cases.
I think, some day, I'll hang them from the clothesline
like a church bazaar of the hints that I've let lie
and watch them, dragged from their drawers and closets,
stick their tongues out as the neighbors pass by.

Where the Pines Groom Heaven

The orchard, aunt Thelma said,
was a hubbub of blooms, like delivery boys at a funeral.
The petals *aahed* with rose-white, breezy mouths
and, tumbling, fell lamentless to the grass.
The congregation with their beaks announced the loss.

And over the riverbank–yes, I was mad again–
as I hid among the wild grape and the slippery elms,
watching the penitents, clear of the reeds and rocks,
shout *hallelujahs* while I picked up my want
and ran, clinching a boulder in my arm to the water

flailing in the mud to kiss death's forehead.
I interrupted, needless to say, the baptism.
Why, child, was April a deranged redemption
and why was May without salvation or a sacrament
except maybe for a rock

when for a month I ached for the angels' wings,
which went and came again in white streams, there
on the highest peaks, where I wandered
in the March wind, longing to kiss God's mouth
as He swept by in the showery mist.

The Sanctified Lizard

As sharp as aunt Thelma is, her mind does wander sometimes.
    She stopped talking about the Bible and after a
    minute was chuckling about great-uncle Thomas. He
    had hardening of the arteries or something and when
    she'd drag me over there for a visit he'd be
    sitting behind the stove pecking on it

roasting in the heat and burning his fingers, and whenever
    she'd walk by he'd shout *You sanctified lizard!* He'd
    go to the toilet and end up trotting down the road,
    the feisty devil. Come back! Come back!

Sometimes he'd back his red truck out, trying to get away.
    Good thing the battery run down. Aunt Thelma told
    me to hush my laughing. Didn't I know it was
    disrespectful? She giggled and opened her Bible.

Going to Israel

Aunt Thelma said she was tired of blaspheming and wanted
       to go to the Holy Land. She drug me all over the
       house with a pencil and paper, listing furniture she
       could sell–walnut beds and bureaus, dressers with
       slabs of marble, rocking chairs, pie safes, armoires
       and books printed in Texas.

Finally I stopped her. I told her she didn't want to go
       to Israel. Some Palestinian would probably drop a
       bomb on her head. She slumped down in her favorite
       chair for sale and cried.

Sister Charlene

Sacrifice the Moon

My sister Charlene toweled her hair,
smoothed on suntan lotion and stared at the Atlantic.
Think of the Pentateuch, she said, and the crazy law
which doubled the number of days unclean for daughters,
and priests so jealous of their pile of rocks,
and so fanatic, as they flapped and squawked over sacrifice,
that I'm still afraid, and rush to the child,
who shies from the lap-wing of the gentlest wave,
and catch her in my arms, sea-anxious, in delightful wails.

Is righteousness, in any case, so bloodless an affair
that I should cringe and pull the towel across my thighs
in this month's ripening crescent of my little moon?
Or sigh for the mustache on your lip, or envy,
as I brush with my fingertips, your manly nipples?

It's men, you understand, who ate the crazy salad.
It was God cast woman shoreward on a floating shell
and men who walled the gift up with the oil, the garlic
and the hearth fire. And in the late millennium think of her–
and Charlene yawned, stretching her arms above her head,
her breasts cupped and firm–a slattern on the serpent's knees,
yet enshrined in a holy niche for all to see

her face a various gold and rose and blue
as the sun moved on the windows so worked in bits,
so buttressed on the sky, that she, in God's great cavern,
was the matron in a chaste caravan.
Children came, of course, and those whose famine,
whose sores and wounds her wooden hands could reach,
when mercy was a profit the bishops reaped.

All others came to a sty, or to a nuptial bed
in which her cowl of innocence was surety, a rewarded bid.
My daughter and her pretty, her homely kind,
unlike the generations who gave what seemed their souls away,
wrapped as a luscious fruit, and wept for the core,
these children won't, as the sermons call for–
and she smiled, tousling my hair–they won't blaspheme
       God's love.
They won't be shackled, moon-heavy, at the shore.

It Didn't Come from Hallmark

Charlene came in and closed my book, telling me there
        was a time to think about nukes, your flesh rotting
        off your bones while you puked at one end and
        diarrheaed at the other but not right before dinner.

I love her inviting me to eat but tonight she was quiet and
        when we finished we just sat there over coffee with
        her touching the roses on the table.

I said I loved her and she told me that was natural out of a
        younger brother, especially when the older sister was
        as intelligent and alluring as she was, and she put on
        some hauteur and drank her coffee like a baroness.

I told her to quit acting stupid and I couldn't help the tears
        coming to my eyes. I want to be with you all the time,
        I said. I don't understand it and I can't stop. The
        only time everything's all right is when I'm with you.

She said she bet that was the way a little boy felt about his
        Mommy when she tucked him in bed. I told her to go
        to hell and slammed my fist on the door, crying, fumbling
        to get out when she put her arms around me and stroked
        my hair.

After a long time she said that pretty soon I'd find a love
        with more than tenderness in it and then she'd probably
        be jealous. You're my brother, she said, even if our
        mothers are different. I love you, too, but you don't
        want to be a puppy dog and neither of us would like what
        would happen and you've got to go home.

Later on she sent me a strange looking card with a note on it.
        It sure didn't come from Hallmark.

The Disgusted Woodpecker

If a soul could cry out then the body would be a heart
        gaped open and the earth would shut its ears because
        of the horrible shrieks and billboards dripping blood
        on Interstate 81

so the soul is deaf, dumb and blind, like the man who slipped
        from the operating table and staggered through the
        doorways, the little rectangles of light, ballooning
        and shrinking down the corridors until he got outside
        where the heat stomped on him

and when the noisy crowd circled around like a halo of chins
        and nostrils he heard a tapping and saw a red-headed
        woodpecker. My god, he thought, somebody must have
        told me a joke about a red-headed woodpecker on a dead
        oak tree with its limbs cut off at the hospital.

It fell in love with the bosomy figurehead on a whaling
        ship. She was so beautiful that he followed her, tired
        out and hungry over the ocean, but when the white whale
        struck she didn't even open her mouth to scream *Save
        me!* so the disgusted woodpecker flew up to heaven.

Charlene's Ex

Charles can't help it I guess if he's disgusted with women.
      I know he hates Charlene. She aggravates him half
      to death, only he loves her, too. He wants to think he's
      a dude laying it on the women but he's not like that.
      He'll probably marry a secretary at his lawyer's office
      six months from now, about half his age, and then he'll
      be bored and love two women.

This car radio is depressing as hell, he was saying on the way
      to work. I ought to wring its knobs off. Sounds like my
      girlfriend's twang. She's through and I'm forty-two.
      Country 'n' western, very smooth, very trite, the doom
      of *good-bye* and *don't cry.*

Divorce, divorce. Kleenexes for the women, handshakes for the
      men, words I don't even listen to myself, and this
      goddamned radio where the guitar is the wail of throats
      on strings and faces pure in grief beyond any bullshit
      in the lyrics.

The Sympathetic Rib

Charlene's ex, who's as tall as White Sulphur Springs,
his cufflinks peek out at me from his coat sleeves
and whisper about his bank account. To see completely,
he was saying, see totally the woman one calls a spouse,
and not just the nag who caps her tears
in pride's jelly jars in the basement,
her mouth a prune in a white box shouting *no*,
yet in a closed shelf in a kitchen,
her eyebrows raised so the nostrils may parade,
as on despairing hooves, disdain,
her lips staked down so all may survey on her cheeks
a great proprietor of disgust, and mortgages, piecemeal,
of regret–a face abandoned, like a Eumenide in a chair,
on a man's lascivious, wandering path

but her desire, to see it equal any Solomon's song:
her athlete stands before her naked as from a stream,
his torso cold as clay, yet glistening, water-glazed
(a clammy chill against her hand, at first,
then the pliant dazzle of flesh)
from which, with her tender dalliance,
springs a white sycamore or beech,
an appentence for the snail, at the arc-bones of her hips,
to glide, with its shelled room on, all up and down–
but her husband, the prophet and jeremiad in her dream-scape,
plows with his moral salt her charmed grove,
so that she stands on the treeless plain of marriage,
barren as Carthage

to understand that is to ache,
as if the carriage bones were pried in the night,
as if one woke with an image of the heart in a shook cage–
a giant hand, the battering wings, the bloodied down
and feathers–to look at the purplish wound and see the brunette,
the bride's hair, as she lies sleeping in one's trembling arms–
to cry out in alarm the dreadful mistake
that loneliness compounded is a greater grief
than all one's loneliness in the huge gift of God.

Selene's Tea

My aunt Selene, more than anybody I know, lives under
      the surface of her words which swirl from her sunken
      mouth out at me in the overstuffed room like knitted
      life preservers.

Now look here, aunt Selene, I'm only asking for advice.
      Should I fix up Grandfather's old house? I'm going
      to graduate one of these days, and I'm dating this
      girl....

Her lips, that longbow dropped in the gravy, drew back as
      if to pierce me with a charm, but trembled instead.
      I'm an old woman, she said, arranging her almanacs
      and herb remedy pamphlets, and I'm dying.

My aunt Selene's been dying for the past nine years. She
      doesn't die. She sips on tincture of laudanum and
      belladonna and holds seances.

I think she dreams of seance heaven where tables continually
      rise and crystal balls click on like television and
      voices come without megaphones from life.

I do not, she said. I dream of gypsy men with curly hair
      and dark, dark skin. Not like yours. You're too
      white to cry.

I looked at the crinkled paint on her eyelids, and at her
      lashes like hog bristles and in her brown, watery
      eyes. Talking to you is like hollering down a well,
      I said.

That's all right. Here, silly nephew, take my hand. I did; it
      was dry and brown as an onion. I'll tell you what it's
      like, she said, to gain a wife.

The John Deere

I must have written down somewhere that desire is feverish
      like swine flu. Damn! In the old days people used
      the elegant word *influenza* or if things really got
      bad they whispered *consumption* and glimpsed the
      blood stains on the scented handkerchief. For me,
      anyway, I hallucinate bodies out of the weeds.

One time I thought I was done with flesh and was
      walking resignedly toward my boredom. I was
      alongside a field where a man was in a John Deere.
      It looked like a bug-eyed, green steamboat with a
      yellow paddle wheel going backward. I was thinking
      about the farmer's diligence and labor when he
      stopped harvesting his soybeans and stared at the
      trees or somewhere I had come from.

I turned to look at what he was looking at and saw a figure
      or a shadow just behind me and suddenly heard
      everyone in hell rejoice and laugh.

Locked Out

I feel like a transcendentalist who came out of the beer
      joint and panicked when he couldn't figure out
      whether the door he was pounding on was at his
      house on Elm Street or the Methodist Church, and
      the voice shouting *Get the hell out of here!* sounded
      like God but it could have been his girlfriend.

He got tired of beating on the door and, anyway, he passed
      out in the yard and dreamed he was a rock. He woke
      up at dawn, a rocky toad, and croaked at the sun.

Uncle Walter

Uncle Walter Chatting with Wilde

When God adorned the world
said uncle Walter, He surely forgot
to grace the act with a form
men could adore.

According to their kind
they fashion, therefore
creation's counterfeits
and glimpse the Divine intent

in transient bliss: a tenor
with inflections in recitative
evokes a puissance in paradigms of air
then chatters about the plot.

The dancer leaps.
The gesture is an isomorph of musculature
and then his body falls away
mere prancing clay.

The Antiquity of the Muse

What remains, sighed uncle Walter,
after the mind has clapped its wings
and rises in furious gestures above the ground,
wrings them and straggles to the shore where Saraghina sings?
What is her gross, her aged and mythic beauty good for,
when one rages, a feathered fool, by her side?

I saw her, in the sea-island pines beyond the dunes,
in a company of tyrants, emperors and consorts,
of slaves at handicrafts and coiffing hair,
of peasants pruning vines near the chateau,
and plowing near the abbey, of cities and distant hills,
of mills and locomotives, of towers and airplanes,
of bombs and weeping and collapsing steel–
they flowed in the moment of themselves without an aim,
desireless white flames, and I grew icy and full of despair.

If I could see her as the dawn, and whisper
in her finer ear, that *if she were all my dear*,
if I could touch the silken celadon of her blouse,
the damp pearls at her breasts,
or see beyond her stone's pocked torso,
beyond the cracked and gritty pigment of her face

if I could see to the antiquity of desire made whole again
in my imagination, and not such a desperate hope
that children cry to see, where they thought wisdom was,
a grotesque, painted bird afire,
then I would know the law of esthetic longing to the last clause.

Hypocrites of Redemption

I know, you've heard it before, that stuff about beauty being
        a tv commercial, a woman so beautiful you think of
        Botticelli or the Maiden of Chios, of Selket, the Song
        of Solomon–but then there's the feminine douche in a
        waterfall or a cowboy's cocky chaps for a Marlboro or a
        home computer on a butte overlooking Arizona

and what intellectual would mention God without a cough of
        irony, or an outright guffaw. Beauty is an oyster-white
        wall and huge framed orchids and birds of paradise.
        Beauty is decorative shit, and it sells

and weird, in rock songs, how words are slugs on the mouth,
        which you can't say about the knee bones and thigh
        bones–and who cares, anyway, among child martyrs
        flicking their Bics, if it's an honest-to-god
        St. Vitus's dance or stoned idiocy

but when it comes to real beauty, real poetry, well, that's
        different, that's heavy. You can't go somersaulting
        Beauty around with the grace of a Comaneci. You
        can't soar into it like Markova and Nureyev, or open
        your mouth like Freni and Pavarotti and have it pop
        out, a ready-made Verdi

oh no. You have to suffer for it, which is all right, really,
        since logos is the wound on the mouth, but what gets me,
        I guess, is the hypocrisy

as if the heavy poets, uncle Walter included–who's got a
        thing for Charlene, *all my dear*–us Americans, anyway,
        who've heard of Kampuchea, maybe, and Belsen,
        suffering and wailing, who stab ourselves with our pens–
        we're flagellants with a paradise we refuse to die in.

The Only Way to Die

To talk about dying for beauty, good god! Your mind would
       have to wear a shroud. You'd have to cough up blood and
       huddle outside on the fire escape

but some have died for it–Dickinson's carriage ride, for example,
       and Hart Crane, Billie Holiday, Joplin, Hendrix, even old
       Elvis–they knew what the sound was

or what it looked like, as Whistler did with his old lady, and
       da Vinci with his girlfriend, van Gogh's wavy trees,
       Picasso's triangles of mouths

the struggles of van der Rohe and Moore, the oval and the
       stainless steel, Blake and Reynolds, Mondrian and
       Kandinski, the waves of Hokusai, the bamboo leaves
       of Wu Chin.

These hang in the mind without any walls, without nails, and
       everywhere are windows to wail through, all open
       doors to holler out of–and we can exit them, like in
       death

and tell me who, gagging on a Stuckey's sign, or one too
       many Wal-Marts, McDonalds, Sears, has not preferred,
       like Yeats, to be a golden bird or to be, at least, on a
       dark road beneath the lights of extraterrestrial beings.

Not me. I'm afraid I'd fry. I'd rather–I mean, if I'm really gone–
       be a ruby phoenix on a woman's breastbone.

When Your Ego Bloats

Damn you, uncle Walter. Unless you're hit by a semi or
        multiple sclerosis, some fate, some circumstance like
        war, which people can weep because of and curse

unless your mother creamed you half to death with a fat breast
        or a father's belt he fumbles with at his waist like a
        long, leathery, unmentionable, symbolic cock while you
        drop your pants

or just twig lashes, the unexpected ones on the path, minor
        sneers, little put-downs, frowns, *Look at your sister,*
        look at your brother, dear–or maybe a test tube frothed
        in the pituitary, or the one in the spleen got broken,
        which no hands of pity can deal with

but when your ego bloats (and, god, what a pasture of illusions
        it feeds on) and like a gassy sheep, bleats in the
        hallway, or bellows like a bull at the door, foaming
        among the picadors you call your colleagues

or when self-pity films your eyes and all your erstwhile
        friends swim by, indifferent as Jaws, well, then,
        forget it, man.

Unless you're battling the horsemen in the sky, and every
        human cruelty that marches up, unless you're a doorkeeper
        in the house, like cousin Michael, or truly aware of death,
        like Grandfather, then you're merely a god damned pain
        in the neck.

Strange Hope

Strange hope, said Uncle Walter
to think a myth rises like the sap beneath the bark
or glimpse divinity in this spongy weather
among wattles and cockscombs in the barnyard.

I should know better.
It's merely a symbol for a bookish mind
a need, past pain almost
minor as lichen on a post, or a gravestone
like shadows gaudy beyond the firelight

but who are these that skip in the morning sun
as children do with ropes, in a recess of eternity?
Who descends through the wet limbs?
Where are they from
those coming through the bud-haze

the conversationalists of awe
speaking of green descendants from the stars?
What is it unfurling from the leafmold and limbs
out there, where joy and grief awake
and fling away their personification
to dance with an actual god

a god in the black May of the mind
whose perfection is best described by an orient sky
pale silk, and a peach twig, its blossom-shed
and a catbird, silly, blustering on a twig.

Cousin Michael

Juke Boxes

Up in the hollow, my brother folds his arms across his
      chest and leans in the doorway, something like a
      crowbar.

Now I've seen guys whose eyes were empty as snail shells,
      a mouth like a horseshoe nailed to a post, hands like
      an ax blade stuck in a car door. Those are the ones
      I don't hang around with much, including my brother.

Why don't you talk to him? Mom asks. You ought to talk
      to him. I *did* talk to him. I even hugged him once
      when he was slobbery drunk. I felt so sorry for
      him, and he melted in my arms like a corpse moaning
      in my ear, then backed off looking wild. Afterwards
      he would stomp out of the room when I came in, or
      glare like he hated me, the crazy hillbilly.

His motorcycle's high. He screams juke boxes at night
      down the road, flaking purple and red scars, hoping
      for a man to love him but hating cocks. He screams
      and screams like a shredded face in a windshield.

The Club and the Harley

That idiot brother of ours
Charlene grouched.
He stays behind at the table
hulking in his ballcap
twisting his hands in his lap.

He gulps at beers and swaggers
the frightened bully
ridiculous in his brogans
torn levis and smelly shirt.

But as the pitcherful disappears he babbles.
He laughs and claps his grimy hands.
I ask myself: what misery, and whose defeat
as he watches us, silly as ostriches
whirl and leap.

Jack-in-the-Box

My cousin Michael, he's a jack-in-the-box, waiting to scare
      himself and leap to a safe place somewhere else,
      waking up I remember him telling me on a bus out of
      Roanoke. I don't see him much any more.

The last time, like in the dark under a bandaid, he made
      me feel really sad, whispering about guilt and anger,
      swallowing blue pills of them, he said, after he got
      worn out from running. When I went out there to San
      Francisco he sounded close but miles off, like that
      fog horn out from Golden Gate Bridge.

We traveled some, and I got a glimpse of him once or twice
      when he seemed like a lion in those scrubby hills,
      sauntering nowhere in particular, ignoring his backpack
      and being afraid, as if he were charmed.

He shook the gold hair in his mane, drawing me like to a
      campfire while he was burning himself up.

The Confusions of Eros

A note from your cousin Michael. I received your poems.
They remind me of a small gilt statue I've looked at
so often it's become ideal. He stands upright
and she's astride his hips, her legs thrust out behind
and they embrace–crooked knees and elbows, breasts
        and buttocks
of Indian art–but their arms arc beyond their torsos
stylized, as if a freedom mentally perceived
like the fog I used to see in pink scraps
high on the ridges at home
reached through their bodies' yoke into my mind.

I first thought they were dancing
naked except for bracelets and braided waistbands–
small Brahman gypsies–until I stooped to see
at the juncture of their thighs, his penis and her vulva met.
I cackled, like uncle Walter with his bad mind
when a docent group found me crouched and peeking
between their gold legs.

Why a mountain poet should remind me of a gilt work
in the Brundage collection is beyond me, different as I am.
You know, I think, why I moved to Atlanta and the west coast
so I wouldn't shame your brother. It doesn't matter.
I would have moved, again, anyway.

I can't, like you, give substance to my longing.
However sweet its object is to touch
it feels like bronze and marble, which are cold
and have a hollow ring. They fade
and from their sepulchers then smile or sing
like those blind sculptures with the lidded eyes
from the kingdom of Akhenaten.

The finest of the poems, I think, are those about our Grandmother.
I see her sometimes, too, but vaguely, beyond a weedy fence
where she walks slowly, and stops. The cotton print she wears
folds to a lump of color as she stoops down. I wish
since she loved me, that she might rise, a god
all gaudy gorgeous blurred with sunlight
although she merely stands and rubs her back
a withered lady with a hoe, and hobbles down a row of corn.

You see! Your poems have left me maundering and nostalgic.
But never mind. They're very good, with the peanuts and
        cockleburs
and the dirt farmer equal to your judge in viciousness.
You've revealed a drama, there, in which the characters have
        wings
where Self bloats like a sun, and yellow beaks clack on the fields.

I'm envious of you from out here
where I seem to be a stranger in a passionate land.
I've so obscured my origins
that the cautered ends of memory hiss and flare.
Fabulous images cast up a mime
and spark with eerie light its somber ecstasies, and burn.
I wake, every day, half blind and scarred
to live in fright among my flesh and bones.

Tell my parents for me that I'm all right.
And what can I say to you–except your poems are fine–
but talk of loneliness? The sky underground is troubling.
The sun is a bauble, here, and painted on.
I'm ill, yet love-hungry at my table
and want to eat at the desert of human skin.
I would drink lips I am so thirsty.
I dream of a purer love, a purer sky.
It smells like an infant's sweet mouth
gurgling at the wall of the face.
I dream that it's God's sweet mouth on my cheek.

Cousin Michael's Trip

1

In the San Joaquin valley
is field after field of almonds blossoming,
fragrant with the unease of spring,
its sudden breath of astronomy
in the dark-moist

stars-clear in the milky limbs
in the night wind
the twig-leaves barely discernible, fluttering.
They're so bizarre,
the Pleiades and the petals there.

2

A giant,
like a shabby bird,
coarse, matted green,
settles, disheveled about itself
as the wind eases, spring damp.

The leaves of the eucalyptus
flat and elongated, silvered, blotched,
the flaking limbs that hang down in the sun
wind-lift, as feathered wings–
branches rise, sway in the cloud clutter

the languid bronze, bruised silver,
splashing and streaming–
shiver-thrill on my face,
in my eyes,
while the showers glitter
light shattering.

3

Along the palisades are the sea figs
coyotebrush, blue blossoms, lupines
rock cress, yarrow, dock, wild buckwheat–
name on name
the Pacific and the hovering gulls.

Yet the scene is perfect without names.
It is a vision of God as an esthetician
who made the soul a gull, raucous,
voraciously beautiful.

But unfortunately He didn't.
He made it an effort, rather, antecedent to flight,
not soaring forward or back,
but like the ruffling wind, immanent as myth,
the taste of salt in the mouth.

4

With the transformation of dawn
the delicate fog on the hills near Tamalpais
vanishes in incredible blue
and with the weeds before me
the wilderness of syllables–

yellow clover, poppies, cream cups
godetias, red maids, cinquefoils, segolilies–
is the gladness wailing
more various than the wind
the grass leaning, and the weeds

although I sense that
beyond my chittering in the wind
beyond the hills, the hawks and the blueness of the sky
is a roiling brilliance, blind-white and babbling
child atom-fiery, Adamless and Eveless
and without death.

5

Far below the Douglas fir
below the manzanita and hard chaparral
the tanoaks and the grass-beige hills
–trisetum, hairgrass, melicgrass–
the stream descends into the hollow
the birches like long bells of light.

The leaf-shadows waver on the surface
freckled by pollen and the water skimmers.
The minnows flicker, silver-flecked
and the algae is bannered, green-sepia
and the sun-shadows ripple on the stream bed.

A voice scrambles out of its bones
scrabbles over its blood, its flesh
and there
muddied heartbeats on the bank

among infrangible, fragmented domes
in branch after branch of the heart-shaped leaves of the birch
is the joy-hurt
attempting to sing.

6

I hike out to the beach–Drake's Beach–
and think of his astounding journey
sails bellows-white, the bulwarks-heavy ship, stern-square
and peacock men from peacock tiny England.

At the base of the cliffs is talus
the boulder-rubble and struggling weeds.
The tide wears thin the blond, rippled strip of sand.
It's foggy, cold, and the Pacific is a grey, foaming roar.

And when the sun slants through the mist
there is a grayness to it
as if an old film
by an amateur a long time ago who overexposed
were presenting the ocean.

The beach might turn transparent
and come and go on an empty screen
like an interpretation, or caring or belief
which stops that split second before seeing.

Nothing is real in the ocean
or on this beach I've walked to the ends of
crimped by the waves and the cliffs.
In the tide pools the anemones are like small earths–
blue, fragile–set in the dark, watery schist.

I watch the crabs, sandpipers and gulls
and here at the end of the continent I am the alien one
and turn to archipelagos of horizons
to hilly pastures like swaths of silk
to a wind less grating
and restless with the salty mist of death.

7

At home
in an Appalachian field
the weeds (casks of the mind
ray flower, disc flower, composite, irregular
parallel, netted veins)
open without glamour
and in the breeze
have their small fling

see
the blurs, gamboge in the blackness
the vernacular
transfigurations of sun–
that vacuum of photons has come to this
ground sorrel, mustard, groundsels, fleabanes
that abundance filling such small things.

8

With the blasting for coal
I paused, empty as a sleeve in the tall grass
looking at that blackness which we call the mind
how it clicks, aperture, eyelid on the sun
and a butterfly, the blue azure
stilled on a joe-pie weed
became eidetic, visual with memory.

I lay down
and was surrounded by the loose weave of the stems
–chicory flowers, millet, redtop–

and saw how distracted the mind becomes
veiled in gnats
the locusts crying *pharaoh pharaoh*
a goldfinch dipping suddenly and gone

in the cloudless, blank-blue sky
which the mind, then, garners
sun-riddled with leaves, spikelets and brachts
the mind a seed-sack, old burlap.

9

Passive at the edge of the road
the sun as a gold, sweaty headband on the brow
unconquerable

passive as paspalum
the periphery of darkness narrowing the eyes

and the mind flickers
invisible wings about it beating like a hummingbird
the tube of its sipping beak
the delicious blurs, then *blink*
a mimosa blossom
fragrant and sweet.

10

The sunlight, as it washes down the sky
is distracted, prism-pretty as partridge-peas.
The voice rises to it
the sweet opacity of love
but is lampblacked, oil empty
a charred wick in the blood.

But the light, look how it showers, optical, photographic
flittering from jewelweed to wild rose
how the glittering hieroglyphic on the creek
flares on the flesh
and makes the mouth a beak.

The senses so pitched at noon
that when the mind says, commonplace:
some blue jays racketing in the tree

my bones hollow nonetheless–
the prophets rasp *delight delight*
and where birds were
in chase and chatter
burned blue flames.

11

Inarticulate underground
but parabled through the bundles of slim leaves
tall stems and languid petal-lips
clown orange

see, the day lilies hitchhiking beside the road
just easing along without a trunk
without a valise
howdy, hallelujah, nice visit.

There is not utter darkness
but phrases, good fortune on the lips
the wild rose, shy, flirtatious
the leaves tickling my face as I lean
gestalt and kindred in the world

but the mind is tiny
and as it leans to the petals–scant, white–
small as a bee in the yellow anthers
the earth celebrates with a louder discourse
a chorus of apostles from the chlorophyll.

12

The mind backs away
(ah, look at it, old hackneyed Pontiac
the chrome stripe on the hood)
turns from the pole beans, the corn
beetle-gnawed in the sun
the coal piled on the mountains.

I know the colloquial obfuscates
blurs in darkness.
I talked to a great man, once
in San Francisco as we crossed the bridge

(which is elegant, flaw-free
like Plato's silken sleeve across the bay).

We toured the scented shops
and in the waste lots between
was sweet fennel, lupines, chess, teasel, burclover.
We watched the yachts go out in the dawn
white in the blue academy.

13

It matters, now
that I am the obscured audience
responding to the brilliant spurge
a filiation of senses

of children playing in the field I walk through
bright plaids and gingham
the tousled hair
among wild pinks and clover
beggarweeds, chicory and bellflowers.

How innocent they are
a babbling documentary without drama
thriving on it

and I, astronomer in the theater
turn in my seat to see the heliographic
a narrow band of images, a passageway in the dark
the reflective mind
screen of artifice

and it's sweet to cry out to the light
(high, on the highest leaves on the trees)
and to the darkness
a soliloquy, intelligible and sympathetic
in its rise and fall.

How futile the ague of emptiness
how futile the careening Buick.
I have heard the sounds
milkweed, poke, mullein

and the brome leans beside the road
delicate as Chinese scrolls
while cars, like beetles
pass through transparencies of day.

I walk away from the road—
ah, look, earth's radiance in the layered sandstone
on which are lichens, moss, ironwood, beech
then the liquid turning, kindling into fire
the whole creek.

14

The mind, convented
wonderful, the lovely mind—
the causeless joy at twilight

and in the darkening clouds
it weeps with a wealth of limbs
wind-lashed, lightning-blanched, shuddering in thunder
the opulence of cries in the esthetic of branches.

The rain slacks—
it slants through the night and is absorbed
and in the dawn
the pear trees' glittering diamonds of exhalations
utterly singing, flushed, ruddy tinged.

15

And I had thought that the mind, once upon a time
poor thing, had metastasized, gone pulpy
a crown of ganglions permeable to stars.

I knew it when it bulged to the light
when it bloated, naked, in the sun
and the coruscation droned
(hear it at the electric substation down the road
droning and droning behind the silver fence)

but I woke to a plain forehead
and tested myself for a skull.
I blinked at my hungry cells
the vulgar enthusiasm of weeds.

16

In the caves of the heart
the returning and going forth
the foraging blood
listens to the babbling in the hollow

and seeing the coloratura of leaf-surface in the breeze
takes a holiday, minnow-like, ecstatically lightward
and flickers near the splashing, gurgling spillway of the sun
having, for a little while, some fun

but that other voice
roiling out of darkness
annunciates above the dazzling stream
that the blood is uncreate, its own origin
and gathers in dust and stone
furred animal

mere chattering in seraphim, cherubim
a mouth of clouds
blond emptiness of the sun.

17

Pathetic vanity
that minuscule of flame–
the darkness, forbearing with my chatter
ventriloquist of sparrows
mockingbirds

will in its time draw near
frightening is the scythe of its wings
neither angel nor sea spray
and will bring its mouth near mine for the kiss

the final knowledge
cold as the photons in space
and continue
winged blackness.

18

How desperate are the complications of despair.
Beyond the innocence and singing
hovering unrecognized above the field
trembling for its thoughtlessness

above the honeybees at the creek
where I smile at the tiniest animals that drink
and laugh at the butterflies on the cow dung
aghast at the tricked-out
gaudy paradox of their sweet tongues

there is a sac whose definition is the mind
permeable, revelatory
drifting above the field
that quart's eternity of torment.

A man might take the field in his hands
a jar of weeds
peer down at the curious gift
blankly material, exuberant
at what he would make an esthetics of
see spirit-glory in

and know the ingenuous
the hinged jaw of the snake
the dour grin
the gelid eyes of the toad in its face
and know his blossoming and devouring fate.

19

The answer
when I think of that greater world
is the Roettgen Pieta
is angels and streaks of gold
is infants and the azure, scarlet folds of baroque gowns

or that holy name unraveled like a tallith
a prayer shawl into history
which is woven again and again
out of the Pentateuch for predication
prophecy

but our gods are all so starkless, Kali-less
so without the horror of repetition
or the dreadful sensation that the self is a barricade
–desire, memory, intellect–
and that each question leads to itself
neti, neti, Brahma

and that our myths
our muezzins, prophets, saints
our madonnas and their child

are an endless bliss and makebelieve of flesh
whereby that other world, that death is made habitable
distended even, unto nothingness.

20

Out of the opaque
spilling beyond the mind's volume an excessive joy
are the silver glitterings on the grass
the frightening plenitude.

I stumble in its chemistry of sheen
–the musky sycamores, poplars and locusts
thorn bush and briars in the abandoned field
mayapple, moss, the watercress in the spring–

and rise with a limp, stuttering
and make bird gestures to the passing cars
a crippled fluttering which cannot rise
to the searing stars far away
of continual creation.

How dark the green is
–the wild grape on the guy-wires
the broad leaves, the tendrils
the green-angle draping at the power poles–

I could touch the leaves
and the powdery, pale clusters of grapes
as a supplicant, but the power lines
the voices dipping from them–shock, volts of reason–

see how we manage
how intelligence speaks through the wires out of our mouths.

21

What passion is there like the love of God?–
to be like grass along the road
and hear the tread of the world
throbbing in the heart
or like coneflowers which lean to the sun
but do not leave their stems
to touch Him
or like a phoebe on a twig
that when it flits about, some leaves tremble
though the tree's untroubled
and when it flies
doesn't blemish the sky.

What passion is there like that?–
its sweet reprieve from the lamentation
the wailing in Babylon
since beyond the cries
constant, variable, is the hum, tattoo
tabla, thrum–
reach with your fingers, thumbs
sparks, burning, the flesh numb as a volt
and stare, the lightning gashes, burns
burst ear drums
and ash on the tongue.

22

The helicopter
thing, giant, death-dragonfly
a khaki shell and clattering guillotine–
it flies low to the flood-site.

I climb the mountain, repeating to myself
this human death, this flood, this death compounded
evil among stars.

Where are the souls of the dead
the coal buckets of children washed away?
Would you grow roses over them
sericea on the scraped side of a ridge
bulldoze the auger-holes
which look like passages to darkness where they go
drowned, black as slurry
wading through the sulfurous mud
into the oozing, dark auger-holes of death.

Let me go, too! Let me! Let me!
cries the child who was never found
whose soul goes unsanctified
wandering the ridges as howling dogs
as owls
and white as moonlight.

23

Cruel sun
opiate which draws us on
even here, far away in the mountains
fever in our outstretched palms, feverish to touch–
what have you made of the earth, this hunger
a red lump on the plain
the humped shoulders, grunts and snarls
the fangs, the blood on the snout
the chin and mouth–
the hunkering in the brush
the scratched earth
and copulation
seeds, and the grain–
and the kingdoms gained
pyres, flowers and flambeaus
kingdoms and candles
knife at the lamb's throat–
cruel sun

when the final hurt, also, is a star
and whether near, a middling sun
or far and giant as a Betelgeuse
it matters little, as does the cause
since going near is to burn at the source of it
and turning back is to stumble
shadows cast before us like stones
cenotaphs of oblivion.
Tears, therefore, glitter in the sun
and Shiva tramples down the towers
and rivers sparkle as they run, to Jerusalem
and on a lake of sorrow, from the leaf-pads
rise lotus flowers.

24

But it's madness
this painting dust in the road
this evocation of ghosts, divinities across the ocean
this talking to the millet along the path
the spider on the blue, spiked crown of a thistle.

No.
There is a time–lightning split down the trunk–
when the heart reverberates
and I go vomiting in the weeds
staggering with distemper
webby and yellowed in the eyes
lip-flecked with death
dog grotesque.

25

Lying in the field
there is a cripple always in some part
the static jittering through the hands
the fingers gnawed

lips cracked
red eyelids.

It has been hot all day
and the moon has risen
oval
above the frayed edge of the field.

See it
at eye level–apricot, tangerine–
in a blur of yarrows, asters and mayweed
the color of meaning
of hearing the field's outlandish tongues

leaf-mouth, blossom-mouth as the night cools
sighing in foreign vowels while gesturing at the moon
we cannot help you
we cannot help you.

26

Westbound again
and in Tennessee, from a rocky creek
the light rippled gold-grey, lichen-splotched
oscilloscopic under the cement arch of a bridge.
I skipped a pebble across the stream
and a green heron, orange beak and claws
flapped languorously from a slippery elm.

Dingy clouds of tent caterpillars
blighted the limbs along the creek.
The worms suspended in them
wiggled and reared about on invisible wires.
A large orange spider, a crab spider
I think, picked and fumbled at a net.

The katydids and harvestflies, repeating raucously
advertised like hypnotists of sex their small selves
and two ichneumon flies
after several tries on a birch twig
linked abdomens, folded their wings
and butterflies at the stream's edge—
spring azures, red spotted purples, wood nymphs
and tiger swallowtails—congregated on a mat clog.

A rose chafer, a scarab, powdery lime green
outlined in black, symmetrical as math
flew onto my shirt.
I let it crawl on my fingers
and turned my hand several times
then flicked it away, clumsily

and a beetle—glittering, imperial blue—
a purple tiger, lay dead among the pebbles:
the chrinoids—scales, cell patterns in the stones—
and chert, chalcedony, metamorphic—white, red oxide
black, glassy chocolate, bottle green, dove grey

and on the stream were whirligigs
the fin-whir as the minnows leaped
the riffle-shadows on the stream bed
the algae green and gold-brown on the rocks.
The minnows by the dozens swerved and fled
or fluttered quietly
and glittered like the leaf-surface in the breeze
of water birches and the alder leaves.

27

In the Ozarks I found a stream
crystalline, pale green as chrysoprase in the depths.
I flung off flesh, a carapace, a cave
and divested of wings and robe

all but the sun's halo and a message against my wrist
a moment's joy in the wrinkled palm of my hand.

Steel-grey and freckled
a flutter of orange on the caudal and dorsal fins
the stripe on the flank
the glaring black-red eyes and blue pooched mouth–
a spotted bass grazed at my fingertips in the stream
its flanks glittering.

28

In the southwest desert
in the mountains beyond the freeway
I found an arroyo
where nestling in the cholla
in the ash and sycamores
were the mourning doves

and cactus wrens were fluttering
and the white winged doves
in the walnut trees and the acacias.
The sotol lilies bloomed
and lip ferns leaned
among the boulders by the pure stream.

29

America
so much the waste country left behind
and northward–beyond Fresno, San Francisco–
the sun slants through the redwoods, mote-gold
though the air is damp
shade-green in the clearing where I've paused.

The sun is everywhere but here
where the air is chill

everywhere in the tallest redwoods
high above the dew where I am, slouched over
arms across my knees on the spring grass
a patch of it where I'm resting
breathing the April air
sea-scented.

The mist fades from the clearing.
The sun has reached out, hot
this early in the year.

30

Through the rainy mountains–the dripping Douglas firs
the madrone and bay laurel near the headlands
and out to the cliffs in the wind
poppies in the crevices, the coiled white ferns
and the sweet fennel, the watercress in the springs–
such a long journey
to the wringing, faint roar of the Pacific.

It has been as if, excluded from unconscious green
unconscious wings, unconscious heartbeats
the journey has made my weakness strength
as if it siphoned my soul
to water the poppies and ice plants on the cliffs
as if it made me pale
and brought me to the sea mist above the rocks
fatigued and dispossessed me of will
and wilted me as the fronds of kelp
the rootless bulbs are, on the sand
as if it drained off blood, as the pelican
shrunken to its sharp bones, and feather sodden
dragging its broken wing along the beach

and I understand, voiceless as a blossom of sea fig
that it has shown me a delicate and fragile demeanor
as the blue anemones are, in the tide pools
the small crabs in the crevices
that it has brought me to sighs
as the wave-wash sweeps across the bars at low tide
as the sunlight glistens in silver ripples and smears of gold
and I hear the desolation and holiness in the gulls' cries
in the moaning roar of the surf.

Cousin Michael and the Hognose Snake

I saw the metaphysicals react, he said: they looked aghast,
Traherne and Taylor, when eternity hitched itself and crashed.
They leaned on their bent elbows–Crashaw and also Donne–
and shuddered that a shabby field should be the dissonant tune
on their old instrument, that assignable to God was a literal sex–
pods and seeds in a silken weediness–and that a vexed
toad should be the glass-eyed paradigm of His complexity.

Donne shouted: what Reason here? Why six centuries,
from the Romanesque to Saint Paul's, to have God, now,
fall so compounded, so absurdly material, in a paltry three,
that even the ancients, and heathens with their cowed
view of eternity, would sneer at the barbarous altar,
at what we witnessed of a sniveling ritual by that Tartar?

But I'm not ashamed any more, said cousin Michael,
ducking their cracked and dingy halos. It was long ago
that I, in penance, fled to hagiography as the cleric dunce.
I looked at his gaunt frame as at an only friend I'd maimed
by neglect. I attended to him, fed him and bathed his limbs,
and prayed that he'd revive, or whisper forgiveness as he died.

Do field mice die? Do men die? And yet he thrived.
He built up ornate walls, a discourse on reality of vaulted
ceilings and roseate lights; and I, in monkish brown, was astounded
by so much meaning. Was it a dream, I asked. Was I dreaming?

The imaginary birds, when they flew, creating
with their turns such covenants made of air that I stared after,
longing for rainbows on my eyes, sun-misted flesh.
How could I have known that life itself went fluttering
through the artifice, that it flared in golden auras
in the trees, and that death also clamored and sang about me?

Entering the Priesthood

What an odd paradox! said my sister Charlene
who was really angry at Michael
that a love for God should send a man
like an astronaut out there
somewhere, to a sterile moon

one of Jupiter's, surely
since from our own
he'd have our crescent planet in his view
one much too reminiscent
blue, like the sea
and Venus, also, which would bring to mind
the painting of her in a scallop shell
the sea wind in her hair.

The moon, however
is as good as a desert, a mountain, a cave
such men go to
though it's the dark side of the moon
desireless as space and stars
where they practice love–
what holy man, otherwise, looking up at the earth
at the blue, crescent sea
could bear the tides of his body?

Grandfather

When Possibility Is a Gesture

When possibility is a gesture near the heart–
Grandfather said, his hand fluttering like a wing–
a cherubim and seraphim of sighs
who ride as refugees the only cart in paradise, the sun
their choir loft filled with cherries, raspberries
and the honied bee gums

to grieve at a sigh
and at the vastness of the universe
that we are cognizant of it as the mendicant was of Latin
and move beyond our common fields into a mystery we cannot till
and complain of darkness, of distance, and so much light

to lament that the world is vague
a veil which hides or hints at some greater consequence
or that it floats as little languages in our minds
elegant as a diatom, sometimes
or ever young and changeable as the plankton

that the mind itself is but a sequence of small flares
and the earth is symbol-strewn everywhere
its darkness lightened as a dawn through each sense
although the landscape alters by their strange license
part earth and part desire:
moles and sparrows would be lost there

or that consciousness is a house with bare floors and walls
and thought, like a blind child, walks room to room
and hears its mother sweeping with her broom, while she sings
its father planing a door–
with a simpler sense, an odor or sound
knows paradise is round, and watery, and a pretty blue

to complain that we are blind or deaf or mute, or all combined
that the cosmos crashes through our eyes like waterfalls
while we fill ponds and wells
disguise the tumult of every sense–
such grievance is, as in the parable
a phoenix's blue feather in the burnt grass
while the bird has flown altogether.

The Minister of the Jesus Only

Uncle Paul grabbed onto me in the corridor of the hospital.
     I was visiting a hepatitis friend and he was cruising
     the dying, laying on the sympathy trip so maybe he
     could do the funeral service.

Come in here, he said, dragging me into the waiting room,
     have a cup of coffee. I wanted to ask you–and after
     he skirmished with aunt Selene and aunt Thelma–he
     asked me if Grandfather was prejudicing me against
     him.

I gave him my suffering, helpless look, staring him straight in
     the eyes, hoping I wouldn't have to answer his question.
     That must have turned him on because he started talking
     about *the* burden, especially since his visions. Sometimes
     he didn't even close his eyes, he said, they just popped
     in front of his face.

I saw an angel, yesterday, he said, but its left wing was plucked
     and cocked up like a hairy leg above its shoulder. And
     the other one was broken and dragged down around its
     ankles. Its robe was torn and its dick and its–I mean
     its sex parts–hung like a face upsidedown.

Last evening I was praying and happened to look down at my
     hands. Jesus! There was night crawlers in my veins. I
     screeched and yanked my clasped hands apart. The
     brethren thought I was visited by the Ghost.

And a while ago, as I was walking into the hospital, a heart like
     a burlap sack had a peach tree growing out of it and the
     sun was splashing big raindrops, but all of a sudden the
     tree was wilted and peaches hung on it like shrunken
     heads of the ladies in the congregation.

Every day I wake up, now, and my head hurts. My belly hurts,
    too, always full, always hungry, like a dog snapping
    at my hands while I'm feeding it. I look down sometimes
    and I don't understand, like my belly's got a mind of
    its own and hates me. You reckon it's ulcers?

The Winged Mule

1

Grandfather shouted: My god!
That nephew aggravates me, that damned Paul
going on as he does about the Serpent.
I told him to remember that, beyond any mythic tongue,
are the ferns and mayapple, the towering gum and hickory
      and oak.
They, too, can whisper us into consciousness,
to eternities of expostulation all delicate
and to salvation, also, of course,
though yoked to Being like a winged mule.

It isn't sin, the enemy I come to,
no childlike dream of the jackal or corbie,
since they were made to babble of pride and doom
in every snarl and screech,
not animals but signs of a colicky soul.
Looking hin and yon in that menagerie,
I cannot find among the multitude a Satan, death's kin.

What healthy mind would choose an image of shame,
of flagellants in the desert?
I'd rather think the soul were a river of fire
on which the mind burned like a wooden skiff.
I'd cast desire, rather, on a field
and suffer loneliness when a different corn swelled in the sun
and watch grief come,
begowned impeccably with birds' cries.

As much to sigh in spring behind a door,
conjecture the tender grass,
as to escape that
which comes disguised in a psychology of the real.

2

The sun, that old delight of the equinox
(do you recall the *showres soote,* or *now springs the spray?*)
that joy is on the photographs from the telescopes
an ocherous yellow. At the upper left,
it casts flames on the blackness,
an origin too zealous for the blooms
which nibble at its light, and too intense for me,
that distant, greenless reality.

And it's an odd age, certainly,
when the mind conceives reality as itself
and throws geodes and orangutans, oak trees and cats,
in the same sack of otherness,
then yanks them out with a sleight of hand,
with imagination's wink,
and calls the trick the *real.*
It's uncharitable, at least, to the mockingbird
and all such creatures
whose extravagance is an unnecessary delight.

And, too, it's men who think death should be bred,
as with their chickens and hogs and beef,
and their dogs, too, among the quail and possums,
and also their children,
that they should die at war purposefully insane
and ascend to paradise,
to Tycho, and stare at us from the moon.

3

Poor earth,
since every God has had an acre out of it,
and we are left with what?–
the blood and nerves of images from which,
as various as zoology, we rage and sing lullabies.

We fabricate our myths
as immanent as ripe plums in a horticultural mime
the sweet indulgences
when the goldfinch punctuates our liturgy with wings
in a green ghost of horizons—
and yet, what a changeable paradise!
the goldenrod in bloom, just as the sky distracts me;
the dying wasp on the casing;
the silent fires without a volunteer to free with ladders
one twig in flames;
brown weeds that rustle in the wind;
the snowdrifts, the blueing darkness;
and our own personal death.

My prophetic nephew exclaimed
that I was near redemption then.
It's suffering, he said, that ties the Serpent's tongue.
He was so earnest and expectant that I had to smile,
so he called me an infidel
and said I knew no more what God was
than a child with a dozen toys.

I lay like a sick cat on the wellhouse roof,
so helpless I would have died, I guess,
handleless, a calico mop in the blustery clouds,
clabbering the March sun with showers.

I was healed, as it were,
by mice, tugged by their clawy hands,
to a landscape which repeats itself.
They grew blue manes and rearing clouds.
Their hooves knocked flat the gate
and I walked, all afire with green, to my aging tree,
and still, my god, my nephew rants about humility.

Something Else

Nature is all right, really, if you watch out for flies, snakes
        mosquitoes and poison ivy. I mean, Nature doesn't
        give a shit, not really–doesn't hate anybody, doesn't
        love anybody–it's just *something else* and Grandfather
        complicates things.

We're down here visiting like ET. You know, come and gone,
        Close Encounters. We've got this anti-gravity device
        called consciousness. It looks like a giant eyeball.
        I mean *gigantic,* and ugly from a distance, stuck all
        over with everything from prehistoric cave paintings
        to Warhol, from Roman numerals to quantum physics–
        but it's not so bad close up, especially our own little
        close-up part of it

but every once in a while it goes blind, stone blind, and
        deaf, too, absolutely, and down below (you don't know
        what's happening) as if tendrils were growing out of
        your fingertips and your nose distinguishes 63 species
        of wildflowers and your tongue crosses over your lips
        like a popsicle in a skillet.

It must have been something to do with the crotch. Have you
        noticed (you men, I mean) that when you're horny
        your testicles do a little bump-and-grind in your
        scrotum? Check it out, if you don't believe me. I
        don't know what's happening in the ovaries, but
        something down there is shouting *replicate replicate*

and after a while, Bam! It's a supernova in China in 1054.
        It's PCP, Coke, Ecstasy, and you write love poems or
        learn to use the abacus or something and it's all right

but, oh god! what's that swelling down below? Oh, no! The
        children are coming! The children are coming! And
        that's when Nature, that's when something else,
        becomes us.

The History of Compassion

In the arboretum, said Grandfather, quarreling with himself,
I watched my friend, the Hebrew, lean, stoop-shouldered,
hoarse and resonant with history.
He pushed a leaf aside on a bougainvillea
to watch a spider and a frantic fly.
He turned to me as if I were an errant child in my simplicity.
How beautiful, he said, is every race and rarity
and every sensual trace of birth and death;
and yet, with arms as wide as suns,
where is the God that welcomes anyone
to justice, love or mercy?

I turned angrily away, but turned back, shouting:
where is your justice, mercy, love–
the star and the dove–but in a Father somewhere
with property to bear, and a mere book nowadays,
a hearsay of psalms, cruel and lovely,
a crushed flower staining the heart
where much is dark in the Kingdom of the soul
and the Kingdom of the bloody, fruitful soil,
where to gain a Zion is to lose Jerusalem
and the history of compassion ends.

He took my arm, limping from the garden
and at the bench, looked back at my province.
There, he said, where your mind is drawn
is a sourceless dust without a destiny
a house oblivious of itself.
Is the soul a dust mote in an empty house
a partridge or a field mouse
when the hawk has talons in the sun
when the owl has talons in the moon
that it should want for a mouth
to cry out knowledge of its doom to its deliverer?

And in this hour of Zion and of zealots
is not by the covetous the vineyard curst
which brings the wine at a cost of divine wrath?
Where is the psalm of iniquity, of penitence, you ask?
We sat together, pensive for a while, and I replied:
among the stars and leaves are hideous desires
and there we suffer, godless, for our contempt
but might not birth and death, birth and death,
bring us, at last, to a god's tenderness?

The Egotism of Death

It's not for me to tell anybody what's the right or wrong
               way to go about death. Who's to say Donne was wrong
               by calling it a short sleep, though what we're supposed
               to wake up to worries me, since I usually like brushing
               my teeth. Who's to say Paganini was dumb wandering
               around in the graveyard, or Keats' bird flinging its
               soul abroad, or Poe sleeping in a tomb with a corpse.

For me it's having crows' wings glued down on my shoulder
               blades, a black iridescent halo back there. It gives
               me the creeps. I leap up, whirl around, but naturally
               I can't see my own back, and it doesn't do any good to
               look in a mirror. Everybody knows you can't see a
               ghost in a mirror.

What death's really like, for me anyway, is a family portrait,
               which in fact is a studio photograph, about as realistic
               as Washington crossing the Delaware. Mom and Dad are
               sitting on the couch. He's always on the right. She's
               on the left, a head shorter than he is, one hand on her
               lap, the other resting on the shoulder of the youngest.

That's me. My brothers and sisters are ranged behind like a
               corona of molecular biology. Grandma and Grandpa are in
               a photograph on the wall behind us.

What I'm doing with a wide-tipped felt pen is inking everybody
               out. I don't know I'm doing it but I'm doing it,
               blacking everybody out, all those I love, all those I
               hate and despise. There's nothing left in the picture
               but me and a couch-arm. I'm in a little rectangle, a
               casket, a tomb, all by myself in the lower left. I'm
               the only one in the gold plastic frame with cardboard
               felt on the back, and that's that.

We Lapse into Wisdom

As if explaining to me, the idiot,
Grandfather said that rapture is unconditional
and isn't bound to a Brahman or a Hebrew caste,
a lotus flower, a minaret or a cross,
but is free of all dogma,
as when, stretched out in the soybean field,
the man I hired gazes cloudward,
oblivious of wages.

When we discover that other sun,
when, through the flecked black of swirl-chaos, we know,
we understand, then we are blinded by our awe.
We blunder like a clayey wind,
and pull green shadows about ourselves,
till we can see our fingers, hands, our limbs,
beasts, trees, the birds and sky–
then cry *This is the light! And this, and this!*
and sing again, like children, everything into being.

But in the west that innocence we haltered and maimed.
Those children dance in the minds of multitudes
but, like a handclap of delight, ecstasy is an echo.
It was shouted from a mountain long ago.
We dressed it with gold and hid its flesh with contempt,
though now we've fallen away from the practice
of that worship.

And odd, for the Hindu imagination,
how earthly love befalls their continuous gaze
as a passionate breach and a baffling of rapture
though they confess to whom they owe their saintliness
that it comes by duress of suffering: a man and a woman,
the seeds they sow, birth and death, and perpetual change.
Thank god, when we are young,
we do not understand what it is the birds sing,
else earth were human-less
and every rose need sigh for itself.

84

The light, however, is not the sun,
though perhaps some origin similar to the sun,
as physics is to a hummingbird or a moth,
as chemistry is to an apple.
But we need, with the convolutions of the stars,
and injury and age,
a closer wisdom than the sky provides.

Much like the bean hulls after harvest,
their scraping along the fence in the wind,
we lapse into wisdom;
and in the hollows of the shells, in the dry veins,
we know what will remain, and what returns

though I wish, sometimes, that, like the seeds,
we had a mask which might, in mercy,
stand the constant testing of reality in our stead,
so that the wings which lie against the flesh,
like sprouts and tiny wings,
might escape into the light at death.

But like a burdock, I stray on another coattail.
If on a branch or plain,
when the first glimpse of creation is divinely gaped at,
when we sing *Rejoice! Rejoice!* and pile up temple walls,
when we leave what we've named behind
and die outright into our paradise,
without a hull or sprout,
without a mouth to form our *hallelujah*,
then not a bird or beast, not a leaf will turn,
not a blade of grass, from gazing at its ordinary sun.

Blake's Little White Boy

Raleigh Airport

You might call it an epiphany. I don't know. I'd only slept
        four hours in the past thirty-six, had a hangover and
        was on standby in the airport for five hours and the
        flight I might or might not get to Denver was late,
        besides everything else

and I was reading a book about another of life's paradoxes,
        this one having to do with how, as symbolic animals, we
        inhabit ghosts and ghouls and nightmares of distorted
        reality, on one hand, while on the other are angels, God
        and everything beautiful and while, I suppose, if we
        had a third or fourth hand we'd juggle levers, wheels,
        pulleys and the internal combustion engine

and as I was thinking about all this very hard, very intellectual,
        the waiting area filled up, though I didn't notice, really–
        it was more like one minute I was alone and the next
        minute I was surrounded by people

and I wondered what sort of symbols, what sort of dreams they
        rolled their eyeballs up to as they walked around, or
        in this case, sat around staring with white eyes like
        zombies in a horror movie and maybe, if we all stared
        upward at the same symbol, there'd be peace in the world.

I could tell I was beginning to fold, drop away, skitter with
        the metaphysical D.T.'s, and thought maybe if I concentrated
        like a bourgeois novelist I might shape up, straighten
        out, and maybe even get to Boulder, although I wasn't
        so sure any more about the Naropa Institute.

I looked around, but it wasn't bourgeois at all. It was more
        like huddled, affluent masses or humanity anywhere which
        suffers Being, for the most part, in the boring wasteful
        holding areas, at Gate 3 or 45 or whatever, with wrinkled,
        tired dignity.

Suddenly I wanted to hug them and kiss them on the cheek. I
wanted to comfort them and tell them it was all right, but
of course I didn't. That'd be just another rolling of
symbolic eyeballs, not to mention assault, molestation
and possible rape of the general public I'd be charged
with, dragged off between two security guards with my
skull cracked–forget that.

But I did listen to the kids, to their thin, sweet voices–white
kids, downy white with strawy hair and blue eyes.
They were beautiful, even when they quarreled and
sulked. I thought they were angels–thin, little-bodied
things with big heads and big eyes.

One of them bumped my knee, and I was so far off seeing him
as an angel that I jumped and scared him back to his
seat, and that's when I noticed the woman gazing at me,
a black woman, young, in her thirties I'd say, and
matronly, although she was very beautiful.

What I figured was that, out of boredom and idle curiosity,
she was looking at everybody and I just happened to
catch her at it, but she didn't stop looking at me.
She never moved. She never blinked as far as I could
tell, but sat there with her hands in her lap, prim and
adult and straight-backed

gazing at me with big eyes and a faint smile, sexlessly
beautiful, compassionate, like my mother Gaea just came
to life and I couldn't stand it.

I had to look away or I'd fall down and worship her and
she'd think I was crazy. Also, I was afraid she would
light a cigaret or take a Harlequin Romance out of her
bag and I'd be dragged down, back here, goddammit,
where everybody frowns and worries, nervous and sweating
most of the time, like spirits rushing with white eyes to
their gates and rising skyward.

The Fever of Every House

Grandfather frowned, a bourbon in his hand:
I believe you think, he said, that I'm steeped in melancholy,
like a tea bag in a poverty of wit, and that, like the coos
of lead-grey, snowy pigeons under the eaves,
I lull to sleep the fever of every house;
or, like the hound behind the stove,
I shift in thought until a motorcycle, roaring awake,
shatters my contemplation at midnight.

What troubles you? That I teach, that I value literature,
that I'm towered in that yellowed, ivory cliche?
Is it these recent deaths in the news, the literal children?
What is it we're to do? Are we to weep and maunder,
or put our hands to our ears and close our eyes–
the mushroom eyes, the whorled ears of the cabbage–
and shrug at the commonplace anarchy of the day?

Or, rather, should our savagery ignite and burn in imagination?
Should we imitate the killing,
trace terror like a bloodhound through the brush,
until we find that bastion or labyrinth wherein, with half an
        ethical will,
the bestial in ourselves wails ecstasies?
Is that too literary a view, perhaps?

But I apologize for my sarcasm.
I believe that literature is the ultimate truth,
the only mirror we can look into, the only reflection
of our blood-stained terror, and live. What citizen,
what parents anywhere, if they could see, would behave
as the Valkyries, or the Olympians above Troy?
Who would choose gloved iron before a child,
or choose to cast themselves, helpless with righteous swords,
upon the schoolyard?

The Blameless Sun

Me and three of my buddies, after partying all night, watched
      a perfectly beautiful (except for a little smog) sunrise,
      the same that's been around for a few billion years. But
      Radio, that asshole, squatting to twist his big toe and
      scrape the gangrene off his heel, hollered in a news spot
      about the black unemployment rate, the Republican debates,
      the depression in U.S. steel, the 400% inflation rate in
      Israel–well, shit, there went the dawn.

And Travis Viceroy, TV for short, nearsighted as a bear, fell
      into the satellite dish, over the lawn chairs, waving his
      hands in the air. He can't talk, otherwise, the fool, and
      there was Belfast, Afghanistan, El Salvador, Libya, dead
      whales, acid rain and bloated babies on the African
      plains.

It's a wonder the sun moved an inch. Why should it, with TV
      babbling, the son-of-a-bitch. And Telex, or Teletext–
      whatever–I forgot his name, stuttered on about Shiites
      and Sunnis, Hindus, Sikhs, Moslems and Christians–
      damn! He was worse than a submachine gun.

In front of the tv, who in the hell am I? Who is it listening to
      the radio? Didn't anybody die before *The New York
      Times*, no Hundred Years War, no flooding of the Yangtze,
      no plague, no Gethsemane?

Why look at a rose in the yard, and knowing the world's worth,
      turn chafer, devourer of life, petals of days and years,
      all that is blamelessly beautiful, and with embittered,
      glittering eyes, like a stupid bug, watch the sun rise?

Like One Indentured

The wind across the grass
the sparkling green-blue swell, Grandfather said
it never cups like a wave's wild crash of sympathy in the mind
but stops, gently abrupt, as the grass endlessly stands up.
Can one fly from the multiplying of blades
and perch like a cowbird on a thistle
tilting and fluttering in the field?

This endless shackle, what is it?
Have I grown act-less, or old with a rusty saw
to suffer mortality with a sigh–
like one indentured, paying with days and years
that little leaves and petals above the pasture
hold me in lien?

And for all my guile, I am an innocent among the leaves.
A touch stuns me, and yet the hand
which hangs in ignorance from its friendly arm
I, poor man, would be blessed by, kiss its five mouths
I am so hungry for bliss–
or else, too bitter for equanimity
scrawl letters of wrath which squall
toy-deprived, like a slobbering mouth–
how could I help that?

But it is time to put all questions past
whether death is blank or foliage with tongues
and to climb down, rung by rung
through the cloud-strewn litter of our canopies
and walk as angels, aged friends in a garden you designed
who made the sun a golden twine on which to hang peach blossoms
and the tendrils of the grape vine.

I know you smile.
They are inveterate with me, the small conceits
just as your habit is, to treat me childishly.
A trellised sun is none the worse than a scold of affection.

But I can't start again.
I am as ignorant as the scalloped galls on the peach bark
but you are mute as the trees and sky, despite all mockingbirds
and deaf, although the twigs push out their ears
and blind as the wind until we touch, oh my friend
and exclaim while the petals tumble down, *ah see!*
and grant to death some little beauty.

The Executioner's Chopping Block

It got so I finally had to cut the quadraphonic's head off,
        the tape deck, the VCR and the television's. They
        were like royalty eating off me out of a pizza box
        with about twenty friends who smoked my dope,
        drank my beer and crashed on the floor like
        boulders in sleeping bags.

So I drift around now without any heads in the living
        room, but being lonely and such I put in the cigar
        boxes with the butterflies. I'd like to fix up
        Grandfather's old house, or build a new one,
        probably a tent with a portico.

Other Books by Victor Depta

The Creek (Poems, Ohio University Press)
The House (Poems, New Rivers Press)
Idol and Sanctuary (Novel, University Editions)